The Beehive

The Beehive
By Talia Coeshott

Copyright © 2020 by Talia Coeshott

All rights reserved. This book or any portion thereof may not be reproduced or used in any manner whatsoever without the express written permission of the publisher except for the use of brief quotations in a book review or scholarly journal.

ISBN: 978-0-578-62937-7

www.tenderlovingcareandco.com

For
those who made me feel *broken*,
those who made me feel *lost*,
those who made me feel *unworthy*…

Thank you for helping me *find* myself.
Thank you for helping me *fall in love* with myself.
Thank you for showing me the *beauty* in pain.

Acknowledgements

For everything you do:

My family
Chris and Lovely
Ron

Thank you.

Instagram: @taliacoeshott
Email: contact.taliacoeshott@gmail.com

To those of wondering eyes,

I did it! I published my very first poetry collection and I feel so greatly humbled to be able to finally say that. I am eternally grateful for every bump in the road, every amount of rage, even times when I felt that my insides were crushing me from the inside out. There was a point in time where I felt that I had all the words for what I wanted to say, but it never seemed enough to paint a picture of the intensity of the emotions I was feeling. This left me filled with a mind of unfinished thoughts entrapped in some sort of prison with no correct way of surfacing the light. I had become numb.

And then I picked up a pen. I scribbled words of nothing into my Moleskin, writing every single feeling down even if it didn't make sense. These poems are proof of the ups and downs that come with love, heartbreak, despair, and anger.

These are the words that have yet to be spoken into existence. I have written, read, and recycled my finished thoughts into a closure I never thought was possible.

I am now able to love myself more than ever before. I have learned what it means to hate the reflection in the mirror. I never thought I would be able to love the body that I have been placed in. But as time has gone on, I have fallen in love with the girl that has tackled every obstacle to conquer her. The girl that I used to despise found a way into my heart by proving that your past experiences do not define you; it's what you make of them that does.

I hope that while you read these poems, you envision a picture of that which I felt a simple sentence could never truly depict.

Peace and love always,
tlc.

Beehiving, v.

The action of overthinking;
Your mind is a beehive, many thoughts weaving in and out uncontrollably, trying to make sense of the craziness unknown to the outside world.

To make sense of thoughts, transforming emotion to words are comparative to the bees buzzing about one by one, leaving the mind and being spoken into existence.

The physical words are only what you allow to be said; what is kept inside the mind is unbeknownst to everyone.

-Talia L. Coeshott

To the Monsters I Miss

I can write my wrongs down
on a piece of paper
and apologize to my angels for letting
my demons get the best of me.

But truth be told,
I am living in a circle where all things are
connected
and choices are turned into decisions
that are turned into tomorrow.
The question is whether to change the present
or
to let it be,
because what you choose to change
can easily change your future.
But does it really,
if all things are destined to end up the same?

I can out-talk topics that have no color
and have faded
because it is a way of coping and realization.
It is not something much
commonly understood but something
that is rather told to let go.
But to let go means to pass by,
and what if I do not want to pass this by again?

And so I lay the bright colored paintings
out in the sun until the sun itself
fades the colors to grey.

Everybody on this planet is
programmed to make mistakes.
We hurt each other because we hurt ourselves
and so why is it that we seek forgiveness
in ourselves and not others?

All good things are appreciated for
a half-second.
However, one bad, much like a child,
can be careless and run all over
the whole garden that took years to grow,
which is now destroyed in much less
than of an instant.

It is tricky to decide between
a want and a need because
sometimes what we want is not what we need
and what we need is not wanted.

To better yourself,
to strengthen yourself,
must mean to be torn down and broken.
A wound feels like an eternity.
It is visible,
and ugly,
and vulnerable
to all who encounter.
But to scar shows strength and thickness
in the way that can never leave you,
yet be the constant reminder of what you have done
and where you have come.
No wound is wanted, but needed in ways
most do not understand.

To the monsters I miss.

Flashback

I knew I loved you
the moment you held my face,
your eyes so lost in mine.
My mind never dared to allow
my lips to say the words
my heart spoke.
A tear escaped my eye
in fear that your heart fail
to adore mine.
My lips found yours like
its sole purpose was meant
for kissing you.
You drew back and said,
"I do too."

Unanswered Questions Pt. 1

You used to point out
all the reasons why
you fell in love with me.

Did they suddenly disappear
the moment you did too?

Liar, Liar

Although the words left my lips,
               I did not believe them.

Countless times I've reread
the words in a book
with the hope that
words may be undone
and rearranged into
perfect endings.
If a fraction of a
tormented language
be different from the last,
may each flower amount
to an infinity of gardens.

But the past cannot be
rewritten
and neither can we.

Deceive Me

I fought for the both of us
because you never would.
I wonder if I had known that
that was the reason
we were destined to die.
Because,
you never cared much
for late nights or staring at the stars.
You only cared for the stars in her eyes
and the late nights where
her lips intertwined in yours.

Enter my mind and try to come out alive.

I dare you.

Fake it Until you Make it

Let the world think
you're the strongest individual
to conquer,
although you're standing on the edge,
fearful of f
        a
        l
        l
        i
        n
        g

        d
        o
        w
        n

Stay a Bit Longer

The sun and moon
taught me that some things
shine brighter when they are apart.
And if they get so lucky
as to meet one another some day,
they'll admire that moment,
but only for a little while,
because
the most beautiful of times can never
last forever and,
like everything else,
must have its end.

You are a face I could never forget.

Mental Notes from the Hive Pt.1

Nobody gives enough credit to the people that are trying to be okay. You go through the day and move through the motions just to distract yourself from the commotion in your head. You're only one sunset away until you find yourself staring at the ceiling with your hands above the sheets, left alone with your thoughts about how to survive the next day.

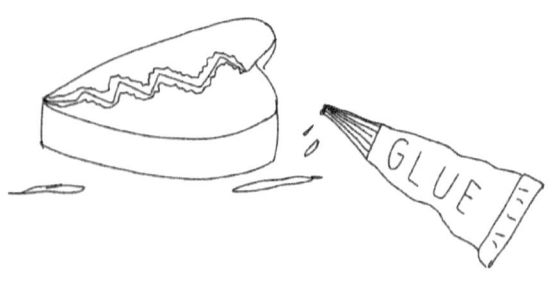

I never understood why we crave love. To love, is to have loss. So why do we pine over what we know could hurt us?

Maybe we just want to feel something, even for a little bit.

Kiss me like you play piano.
Soft and gentle.
Hard and fast.

Entice Me

Why does my heart speed up
at the mention of your name
or
the slightest observation of
your notification on my phone?
It feels as if
I am buzzing with electricity.
I cannot breathe
even though my chest is moving
up and down,
rapidly
and
I kind of like it.

It Had to Happen Sometime

I know you are the fuel I need
to ignite my fire,
but the only way
that can be a reality
is if we burn.

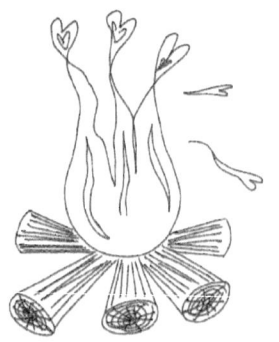

I looked to your big brown eyes for the love you always promised me.

My Foolish Heart

You lie so pretty.
I wanted to believe your words
through and through.
But
I can't call you a liar
because
I lied too…
By telling myself that was something
you could never do.

Too many times
I let apologies
be written off
by words.

Collision

We collided like the waves
on a perfect day.
We were everything that
could have been beautiful
until
we crashed and faded
into nothing.

Darling,

Pull me in close and bite my lip.

Dependent

Don't
pour your half of the glass
into mine
trying to make me feel
like I am enough
because
I'll spit it right back
at you and we'll
find ourselves
half full,
unfulfilled,
once again.

I thought that
you had broken my heart,
but instead have reminded
me just how much
I am able to feel.

Unanswered Questions Pt. 2

I wonder of all thoughts unsaid.
Where do they go?

*Everything is
simple.
Black and white.
You just made
things
grey.*

Time Travel

I would like to say that
I miss a time when things
were simpler,
but things were never just that.

Simple.

2 or 3 or 4am

You didn't ache for me
when your shirt hugged my back,
when the night whispered,
"love,"
when a hole in the shape of you
rested reserved upon my chest.
Now your hand calls upon
the hairs on my neck, lingering
the sting of an,
"I miss you,"
and lust on your lips.

You called my scars
beautiful and
begged that
I make you
one of them.

Mental Notes from the Hive Pt.2

I've fallen in love and have lived so many amazing moments. So why do I not remember the details that made these moments so great? I remember the bad times, however. Every single detail.

Every single one.

Loving you wasn't enough.
I should have left you wondering
what my heart's next move would be.
If you were worthy of
my infatuation, my touch,
my devotion…

If an empty space in my bed
meant the equivalent
to my heart's barren chamber,
would you be worthy of fulfilling it?

If I had left you without
the clear answers to my
indefinable love…

… maybe then you would have stayed.

I don't want to be in love with you,
but I just can't get enough of you.

Still,
I struggle to
shut the window
that sends a draft crawling
through the bedsheets that
mask the silhouette you and I lay,
entangled,
untouchable.
Clinging onto our yesterdays,
enabling only the shivers
rattling my mentality,
sanity…
Unable to undo damages
of love lost,
a comfort in the company
of faux hopes…

Shut the damn window.

In a concrete room
painted in upscale frames,
she is the most valuable
piece of all.

I hope you fall in love with her.
She just wants someone to notice,
to notice that she's scared,
not of falling in love,
but of not being loved back.

She's exhausted of feeling *unloved*
unwanted
alone.

Fall in love with all of the imperfections that
she won't even allow others a chance to judge.

Fall in love with her *body*
drive
emotion.

Recognize her pure heart.

She just wants to be *loved*
wanted
held.

I'll lay here and listen
to the
echoes of my own words.

It's as if I felt I could
find my way alone,
but have consumed myself
and all thats left is the drive
I allow myself to have.

Unanswered Questions Pt. 3

How can a heart be so full
and eyes so eagerly wide,
have all the love in the world to give,

yet be surrounded by deceitful lies?

Pain is
feeling every sensation
or
feeling nothing at all.
A static of fibrillation
or
an infinite flatline.
Yelling at the thoughts
in your mind to quit racing,
or
driving in the dark,
listening to soft vibrations.

Love Could Never Fix Us

Pick me apart from the
rest of the people
you eye down in your memories.
Reassure me of my mind,
I feel it slipping and
I need your hand
to cup my cheek.
But even your love
could never heal
the damaged effects
of what used to be.

She loved him with her everything.

He left her like it was nothing.

You treat girls
so different
once you don't
give a damn about
them.

Does Time Tell?

The wound heals,
 but the scars never do.

Face Me

You had once asked me
what my worst fear was.
Who could have known
that I'd be looking into the eyes of it?

You were the rose.
I, the thorns.

How can the two become one when they are not infatuated?

I could say the same for us.
You gave me a reason to breathe
and then took my breath away.

How can my poison be my antidote?

Fuck you.

You stripped off my clothes along with my dignity and I can't decide who I resent more for it.

-you or *me*

1515

Some days I scream at the world
and question my existence.

Some days I question my strength.

Some days I drench my pillow
in a sopping mess of tears.

Some days I hope my bed
swallows me whole.

Somedays I want to disappear.

But somedays,
I don't.

All anyone ever wants is to be *understood* without having to get someone to *understand*.

Who Are You, Anymore?

I thought I could walk
through your brain and
find myself standing
at the end of this maze.
But I found myself lost,
confused at the pattern
I had imprinted to
the feeling of you.
My eyes no longer
grab yours,
our world of an internal
language is buried
among the rest
of the people
I used to know.

Try loving someone
like you know you'll never lose them and
maybe you won't.

From Me to You Pt. 1

So cry. Listen to the song that brings back memories. Look at old photos that were happiness through your hands. Eat your feelings. Binge watch all your favorite movies. Burrow yourself in your deepest thoughts. Scream at the wall until your throat dries out. Play that *sad* playlist. Divulge into your weaknesses. Entertain them, actually.

But.

Don't get stuck in them. Breakout of the funk. Laugh until you cry. Surround yourself with loved ones. Play that *hype* playlist. Take new pictures. Make new memories. That doesn't mean the old ones are going anywhere. Go out, try new foods. See all the new movies. Reflect on your thoughts.

We are all going through things. It's all about *how* we get through it. Recognize. Create your path.

A nesting doll
without its layers
is a beautiful cavern of hollowness,
bare.
I wish
I hadn't given you the deepest
parts of me that
I no longer have
to make me feel
complete.

Mental Notes from the Hive Pt. 3

I can't decide if your words elicit what you want me to believe or if you need to speak words into existence only to hold confirmation of what you wish to be true.

Faux Hope

Maybe it was my fault
for believing in us
when you
didn't believe in us
at all.

Nineteen

She gets tattoos because
she's addicted to the pain.
That's why
she falls in love.

So blue she could paint the sky.

Helios

It's
hard
to
look
at
the
sun
when
it's
blinding
you.

From Me to You Pt. 2

Allow yourself to open your mind. Meet new people and listen to their thoughts even if you don't totally agree with anything they're saying. Find new perspectives and alter your thoughts from aside what is *normal* to you. You may surprise yourself.

Take a chance on change. Be willing to gather further insight on what you may or may not already know.

What could possibly be the harm in that?

You deserve to be told that you are extraordinary.

3:43am
10.05.19

Dear you,

This is the first and final draft I will write of this.
You will not see this until the rest of the world does.
I wonder if you will know that this is meant for you.

I remember seeing the exterior of you. A body with thoughts, emotions, and such a rebellious mind. But no one would ever see that, not even me. We were kids. That's all there was to it. You were this kid who no one knew anything about. Maybe the basics, sure. But the raw side of you remained unseen. I wanted in.

But you wanted me out.

You pushed me to the point where I should have been broken. I should have flipped the page, given up. I refused to let people be right about you.

You were this person with a mask who was in need of someone courageous, persistent, curious enough to take it off.

I fell for you, I really did. I fell for all the things that should have turned me away.

But I took off the mask.

You showed me a world I didn't know existed. Cliché, I know. You showed me love and compassion, and for the first time, I felt those sparkles in my eyes that I've heard so much about. You showed me wondrous nights of looking at the stars, talking about life. You showed me that I was worthy of lov*e*.

I have been damaged. Broken, but not shattered. You slowly picked up my pieces and glued me
together.

I am worthy of love.

I know that now. Because of you.

I don't know what I expected
love to feel like.

I melted into your words
as if they were everything I ever needed.

I don't know what I thought love was,
I only knew your hand,
the only way to slow
the rhythm of my heart.
Your eyes,
all I needed to hear
what you didn't speak.

I don't know if I knew what love was.

I then wonder what I was feeling
when I told myself
this thing called "love"
wasn't worth it.

He Felt like Home

I never thought I could
love anyone the way
I loved you.
I never thought I could
love myself the way
you taught me to.

I broke	Still,
your heart.	you continue
	to break
	mine.

No I Don't

I lie to everyone
but mostly
I think
I lie
to myself.

A Stranger in my Own Home

I am looking in the mirror,
at a reflection of someone
I do not know.

I see sad eyes,
    messy hair.

        a round face,
        snubbed nose.

But who is she?

I see tattoos,
    piercings.

        scars,
        a fib of a smile,
        controlled.

This is the body of my secrets,
                my memories,
                my hopes,
                my thoughts.

Why do I fail to recognize her?

His heart
could
freeze
the sun.

Don't Leave

People always leave.
And every time you've left,
you have taken a piece of me
so much to the point
where I do not know
where I stand.
You broke off my pieces,
one by one
each time and now
I have nothing left
to be broken.
I have crumbled like the
snow falls
and
once I fell for you
I melted.

True Story

How can three words
be spelled the same,
pronounced the same,
heard the same,
yet have such distinctiveness
in meaning?

I care about him.
I love you.

I am in love with her.
I love you.

2am

And as I processed your words
my heart grew warm.
But not the good kind.
More like a feeling of a never-ending
well that descends into
a hopeless darkness and
the only sense of feeling
is the way your
chest caves in when you
gasp for a breath of air
because you've drowned
in the tears that those
words gave you.

Did You Ever?

The worst kind of liar is the one that looks you in the eye and means every word.

Unanswered Questions Pt. 4

Did you mean it the first
time you said
I love you?
And did you mean it
the second, third or
hundredth time after that?

Was is the 82nd time
when the meaning disappeared
or maybe the 54th
or maybe the first…?

I'm left guessing..

Dessert

My teacher taught me that
dessert has two s's
because dessert always has
you coming back for more.
But you deserted me and yet
I still find myself wishing I had more.

Hibernation

Losing you was a different
type of pain.
The type of pain that
you don't even feel until
it creeps up and
rests inside you.

You're a lame
excuse of the
person I was
before you.

Hypocrite

I tell her she can.
I tell her it gets better.
I tell her to always remember her purpose.

I can't.
Does it?
I forgot.

Some days I feel an imprisonment
to my thoughts just
simply trying to survive.

…some days I want to set myself free.

From Me to You Pt. 3

Life goes on.
People grow.
People change.
People get hurt.

Understand

the intentions are pure.

Understand

it is time to let go.

Understand

it will be okay.

Because

Life goes on.
People grow.
People change.
People rise.

Not Your Average Solar Eclipse

My heart sinks
at the thought of
trying to become better
to fit the outline
of the person
I need to be for you,
but
a circle and a square
will never align
no matter how hard you try.

I need to get away from the thoughts
that leave my mind   t   n   l   d.
                                  a   g   e

Mental Notes from the Hive Pt. 4

I am lacking the inspiration that I need to fulfill myself and it's left me feeling empty. I find myself asking questions with loose ends. It's troubling and scares me. It's scaring me of this life in which I'm meant to excel. Who am I to be when I am unaware of myself?

09.17.19

With a pen to my hand,
I watch these pictures
evolve to words,
sprawled on display for
my imagination to run wild.

Call me a Hopeless Romantic

I'll wake up in your oversized tee hunched over my back and attempt to slip a love note on the side table for when you decide to open those eyes that I constantly find myself lost in. You'll catch me by surprise and wrap your arms around my waist, capturing me into the comfort of where I lay. The laughter with mouths opened wide, grabbing your face with both hands just trying to be closer than close to you...

That's what I'll wait for.

I wish saying, "*I love you*" promised one back.

Smile for the Camera

So beautifully sculpted,
the seal between my kiss and
your love,
the silent space between
our bodies,
the gasp of air between my teeth,
your lips
on me and suddenly a moment
is my picture captured.
click
Your name walks throughout my
ears and
one blink is enough
to revisit
the solvent between lips, parted,
the tension of one body ripped
in two,
the breakaway before the goodbye.
click

Alphabet Soup

I'm searching for the
right words to say,
or maybe
just the words
that are worthy enough
to depict the sound wave
of my emotion
and,
maybe I'm just
utilizing the wrong letters,
not forming what my mind
truly wants to say,
but I'm trying,
I'm reaching,
and yet it still doesn't
seem to scream the words…

I need you.
Here.

Find the beauty
in her smile
and
the pain
in her eyes.

You'd Hate to Admit It

The day I had to ask
if you still loved me
was the day
I should have realized
that you stopped.

You showed me heartbreak in its most literal form.

Break Up Sex

Suddenly I'm tracing my finger
along your chest where my head
lay,
rest upon the crevice of your shoulder.
A thought of desired
I love you's
I miss you's
I need you's
secretes my mind, flooded.

I'll let silence speak instead.

The hardest part
about you leaving was
knowing that if you'd
return, I wouldn't be here
when you got back.

Fifty Percent

If I let go of your hand,
will yours remain intertwined?
Will you carry my weight
if I've given up,
press your palm close
and dig your fingernails
into the skin of mine
or will my absence cause your
roots to unwind?

Misunderstood

I am one
all the while I feel I am none,
entrapped in an entanglement
of words unsaid,
pretending to be unaware
of the tragedy ongoing
beyond the window,
through my eyes,
you see.
No one could ever allow
themselves to enter my mind,
for no one would come out alive.

I wouldn't wish it upon the worst of beings.

Am I the dust collecting
upon the windowsill until
swept away?

From Me to You Pt. 4

Like you, like me, like many others, I have my nights where my only comfort is watching the
puddle of tears expand on a white bed sheet.

The only thought to slip my mind is,
"When will it stop? Will it ever?"

The question will arise if it is worth it.
And I am here to say,

I don't know. But there is one way to find out. And it is through those dark moments that you must have the strength to search for brighter ones.

Because like you, like me, like many others,

I have moments where the sky is bright, but my eyes shine brighter. Colors are vibrant and you can feel the life in your lungs.

It might be a game night with your dearest friends and the only thing you hold tighter to your heart than this feeling you're experiencing is the wine glass and laughter that comforts you more than that fluffy blanket
swallowing you.

These moments are infinite.

I can picture a time when things
are better.

I don't know when that will be, or how many bad days you'll have to go through to get there, but there is only one way to find out.

And then you'll know for you, for me, for many others.

Sometimes I drive
to the music that
matches the weather.
I don't say a word,
I let the music carry
the weight of the words
I have to say.

Mental Notes from the Hive Pt. 5

My whole life has become this blackout poem where I try to shine light on the highs of my existence. The lows are always there, covered by a hazy memory, and if they were to resurface, I don't know what I'd do.

The look in your eyes makes the pain worth it.

Mental Notes from the Hive Pt. 6

I'll say you're the one
who must learn how
to open your arms
wide enough to let me in.

You're the one
that doesn't understand how
to feel beams of sunshine
because you're too afraid
of being burned by the light.

You're the one
that hasn't abandoned the idea
of being alone
because..

What if that is
the only option?

I'll say it's you,
that you're the one.
Because it's easier than
accepting that maybe
I'm just not the one.

Mindstuck

Help me find where
my mind wanders.
I'm afraid that I have lost myself
in places where
I do not feel I am
able to recover.
I'm losing my mind
trying to find it.

You've Made Your Bed but I'll Lie in it

I've told myself
at least a million times
that you wouldn't break
me down.
But then again,
you did
because you had
the integrity
of locking eyes
and promising me
that it would always be us.

If I was your everything,
I guess it would be logical to say
that now you have
nothing.

It should make sense,
shouldn't it,
where you should lay,
reaping what you sow?
But instead I remain
in your bed that you've made.

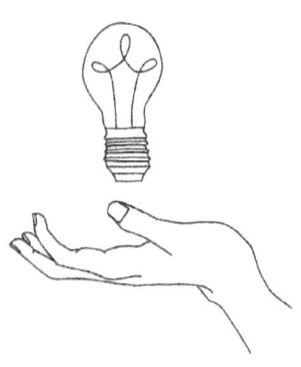

So Close, So Far

Hold out your hand.
I feel as if
I'm reaching for a light
that is not surfacing.
I see you.
I want to feel you.
Believe me.
My fingertips graze the
rigid outline of your identity,
too close to being something,
and somehow,
nothing.
I'm never close enough to
fully consume the wholeness
that I deserve.

I cannot do it.
I cannot do the internal completion
of what I need to be for you.

I will never be her
in any way
and I don't think
I will ever be enough.

When you look in my eye,
her sparkle will not reflect.

And as much as I wish
I could be that for you,
it seems I will have to find
someone that views my
every move as art in itself.

I deserve that much.

Hands tangled
and this time I want it
this way.
I want tied knots and frazzled strings.
Let it take an eternity to
sort out our mess.
Hands tangled
and I'm yours.
Side by side, neat and
simple is where
I never want to be.

Sunday Morning

I watched your wandering
eyes trace my body while
your fingertips guided my
stray hairs behind my ear.

You watched the sun rise,
reflected upon my
honey eyes
and the sunlit shadows
that hid between
the crevices in our
wrinkled sheets.

This was our moment.

Your words mesmerize me,
sweet poetry rolling off
your tongue.

It's a damn shame
I won't allow myself a taste.

Forever is only as long as you perceive it to be.

From the Bottom of my Heart

Poetry is letting the momentum
of the music in your head
flow onto a scrap of paper.
Poetry is a feeling of emotion put
into words, unable to be sorted aloud.
Poetry is letting tangled thoughts
unravel before your eyes.
Poetry is letting the words slip
between your teeth before you have time
to grasp ahold of them.
Poetry is turning the darkest of emotion
into something utterly beautiful,
or enhancing a radiating light.
Poetry is…
Raw.
Uncut.
Beauty.
Pain.
Agony.

Poetry is the language of
my deepest thoughts.

Index

Beehiving 11
To the Monsters I Miss 12
From the Bottom of my Heart 157

Poems about Heartbreak
Rewrite 18
Deceive Me 19
Stay a Bit Longer 24
She's Desperate 29
It Had to Happen Sometime 32
My Foolish Heart 34
Too Many Times 35
Collision 37
Numb and in Love 41
2 or 3 or 4am 46
Not My Angel 47
Loving You Wasn't Enough 51
A Draft is Calling 53
Love Could Never Fix Us 60
Everything… Nothing 61
Surprise, Surprise 62
Face Me 65
Ironic 66
Who Are You, Anymore? 72
Shedding Layers 77
Faux Hope 79
Nineteen 81
Petty Heart 96
Cold Heart 100
Don't Leave 101
True Story 103
Did You Ever? 106
Dessert 109
Hibernation 110
Unknown 111
Not Your Average Solar Eclipse 116

Unknown 123
Smile For the Camera 125
Alphabet Soup 126
You'd Hate to Admit It 128
You Know Who You Are 129
Break Up Sex 131
Fifty Percent 133
Call me Crazy 143
You've Made Your Bed but I'll Lie in it 147
Diet 153

Poems about Love
Flashback 15
Images 25
Love Me 30
Entice Me 31
Honey 33
Darling 39
And Everything in Between 43
In love with you 52
I Hope You Fall in Love with Her 55
Experiment 1 73
3:43am 89
Love or Lust? 94
He Felt like Home 95
Call me a Hopeless Romantic 121
Me 150
Eternal 151
Sunday Morning 152

Poems of the Mind
Liar, Liar 17
Dare 21
Fake It Until You Make It 23
Gallery 54
Fuck You 68
1515 70
Unknown 71

Helios 83
Extraordinary 87
No I Don't 97
Tangled 117
Mind of a Mind 120
I Am One 132
Black Skies 140
Forever 155

Poems about Sadness
Dependent 40
Time Travel 45
Down the Drain 57
Pain 59
Does Time Tell? 63
Blue 82
A Stranger in my Own Home 99
2am 105
Hypocrite 112
Prisoner 113
Symmetry 127
Misunderstood 137
Unknown 135
Mindstuck 145
So Close, So Far 149

Unanswered Question Pt. 1 16
Unanswered Questions Pt. 2 42
Unanswered Questions Pt. 3 58
Unanswered Questions Pt. 4 107

Mental Notes from the Hive Pt. 1 27
Mental Notes from the Hive Pt. 2 49
Mental Notes from the Hive Pt. 3 78
Mental Notes from the Hive Pt. 4 119
Mental Notes from the Hive Pt. 5 141
Mental Notes from the Hive Pt. 6 144

From Me to You Pt. 1 75
From Me to You Pt. 2 85
From Me to you Pt. 3 115
From Me to You Pt. 4 139

About the Author

Talia Coeshott is a newfound poet, born and raised in the Bay Area, who began writing poetry in her Senior Year of high school. Her love of poetry has become an outlet for the many thoughts that have yet to reach its surface. She loves to journal, discover the best coffee shops, admire art, take the longest naps, and read books while lighting one, among many, of her candles. She now lives in Long Beach where she is currently pursuing a degree in Journalism at Long Beach City College, California. In her eyes, every day is seen as a new opportunity to grab ahold of life and demand the most out of it.

Visit her on Instagram at @taliacoeshott
Visit her website at www.tenderlovingcareandco.com

www.ingramcontent.com/pod-product-compliance
Lightning Source LLC
Chambersburg PA
CBHW021952290426
44108CB00012B/1041